Chaos
COORDINATOR
#NURSELIFE

JOBARTS4U

Publisher : Jobarts4u Publishing
Edited and formatted by the Publisher
Source of Graphics : Creative Fabrica

LOVE
#nurselife

JOBARTS4U

MY BLOOD
TYPE
IS
Coffee

JOBARTS4U

NOT ALL
angels
HAVE WINGS
SOME HAVE
stethoscopes

JOBARTS4U

DON'T FLATTER
Yourself
I WAS LOOKING
AT YOUR VEINS

JOBARTS4U

CUTE ENOUGH TO
Stop your heart
SKILLED ENOUGH TO
Restart it

JOBARTS4U

NACHO
average
NURSE

JOBARTS4U

NURSE
MOM
BOSS

JOBARTS4U

Nurse Life

JOBARTS4U

Don't mess
WITH ME
I get paid
TO STAB PEOPLE

JOBARTS4U

LLAMA
NURSE

JOBARTS4U

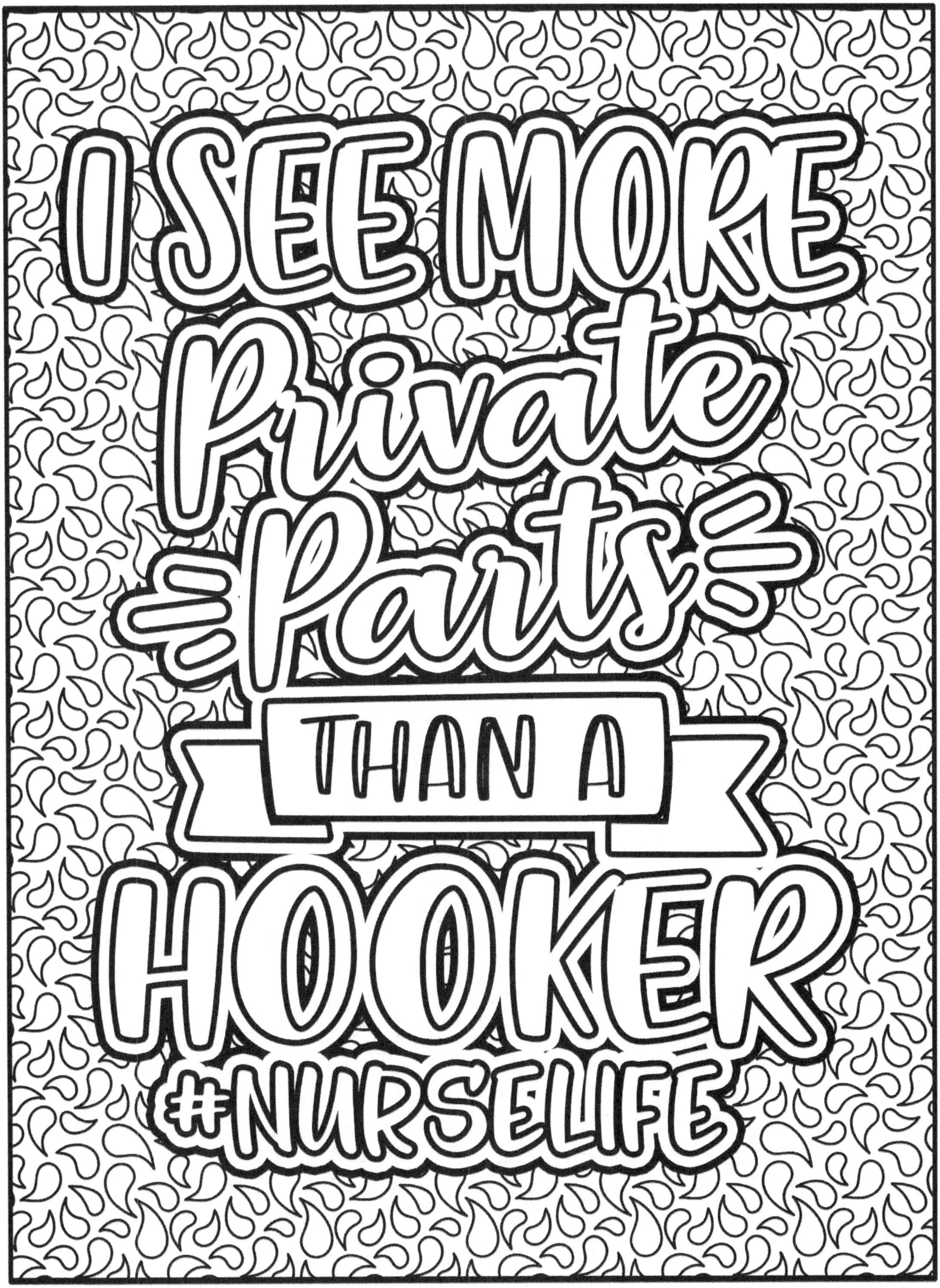
I SEE MORE
Private
Parts
THAN A
HOOKER
#NURSELIFE

JOBARTS4U

Nurse
A TITLE
JUST ABOVE
Queen

JOBARTS4U

FORGET THE GLASS
SLIPPERS
THIS
Princess
WEARS
SCRUBS

JOBARTS4U

NURSE
I CAN DEAL WITH
TRAUMA
NOT Drama

JOBARTS4U

Nursing
IS A
WORK OF
heart

JOBARTS4U

Be Safe
DRINK
WITH A
nurse

JOBARTS4U

EDUCATED
Drug
Dealer
#NURSE life

JOBARTS4U

coffee
SCRUBS
& rubber
GLOVES

JOBARTS4U

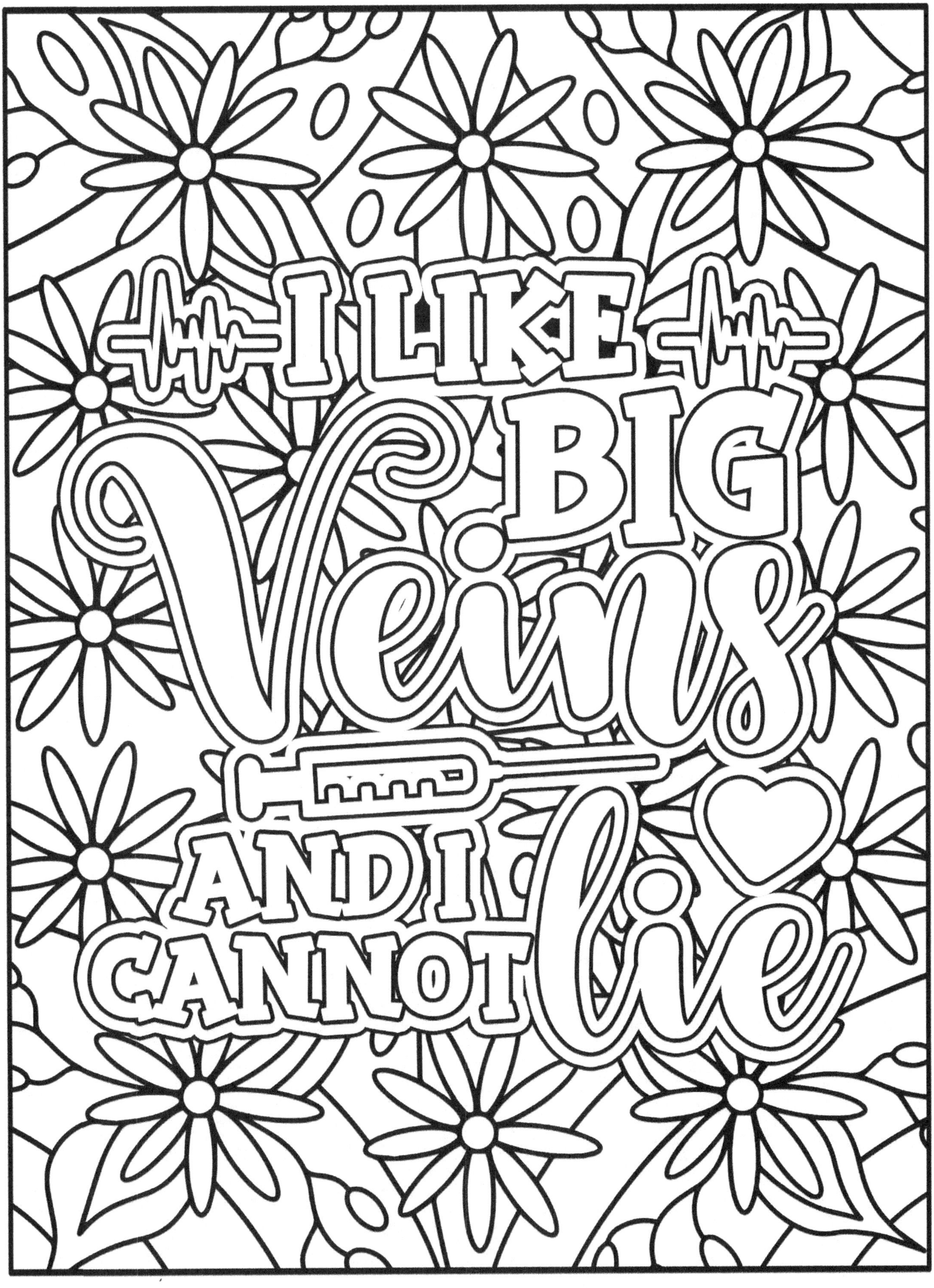
I LIKE
BIG
Veins
AND I
CANNOT lie

JOBARTS4U

Livin'
THAT
Nurse
LIFE

JOBARTS4U

I'M A
Nurse
WHAT'S YOUR
Superpower?

JOBARTS4U

SHE BELIEVED
She could
CHANGE THE WORLD
So she became
A NURSE

JOBARTS4U

Nurses
ARE LIKE
PINEAPPLES
Tough ON THE
OUTSIDE
Sweet
ON THE INSIDE

JOBARTS4U

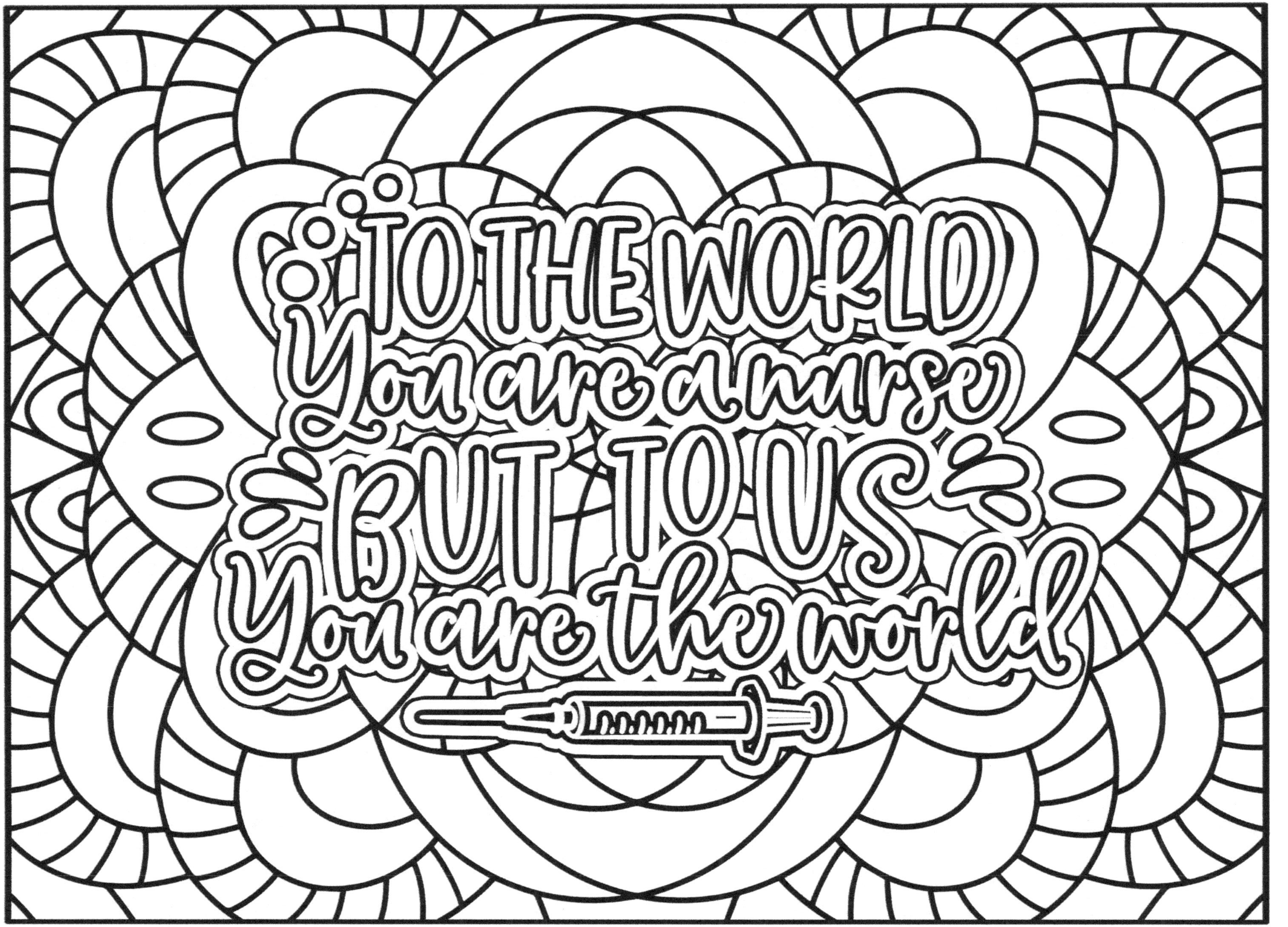
TO THE WORLD
You are a nurse
BUT TO US
You are the world

JOBARTS4U

I AM A
MOM
AND A
Nurse
NOTHING SCARES ME

Nurse
because
SUPERHERO
isn't an
OFFICIAL JOB TITLE

JOBARTS4U

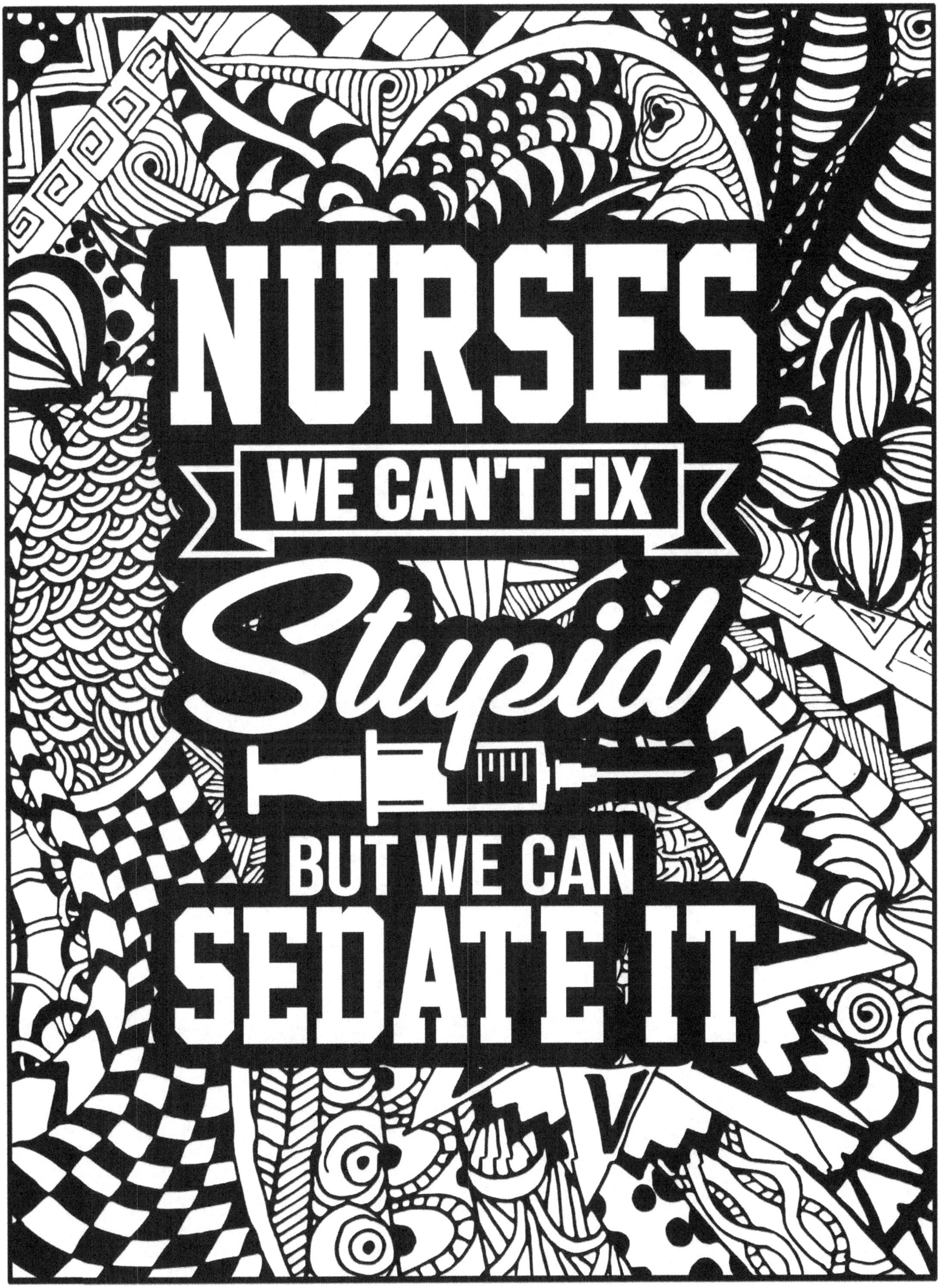
NURSES
WE CAN'T FIX
Stupid
BUT WE CAN
SEDATE IT

JOBARTS4U

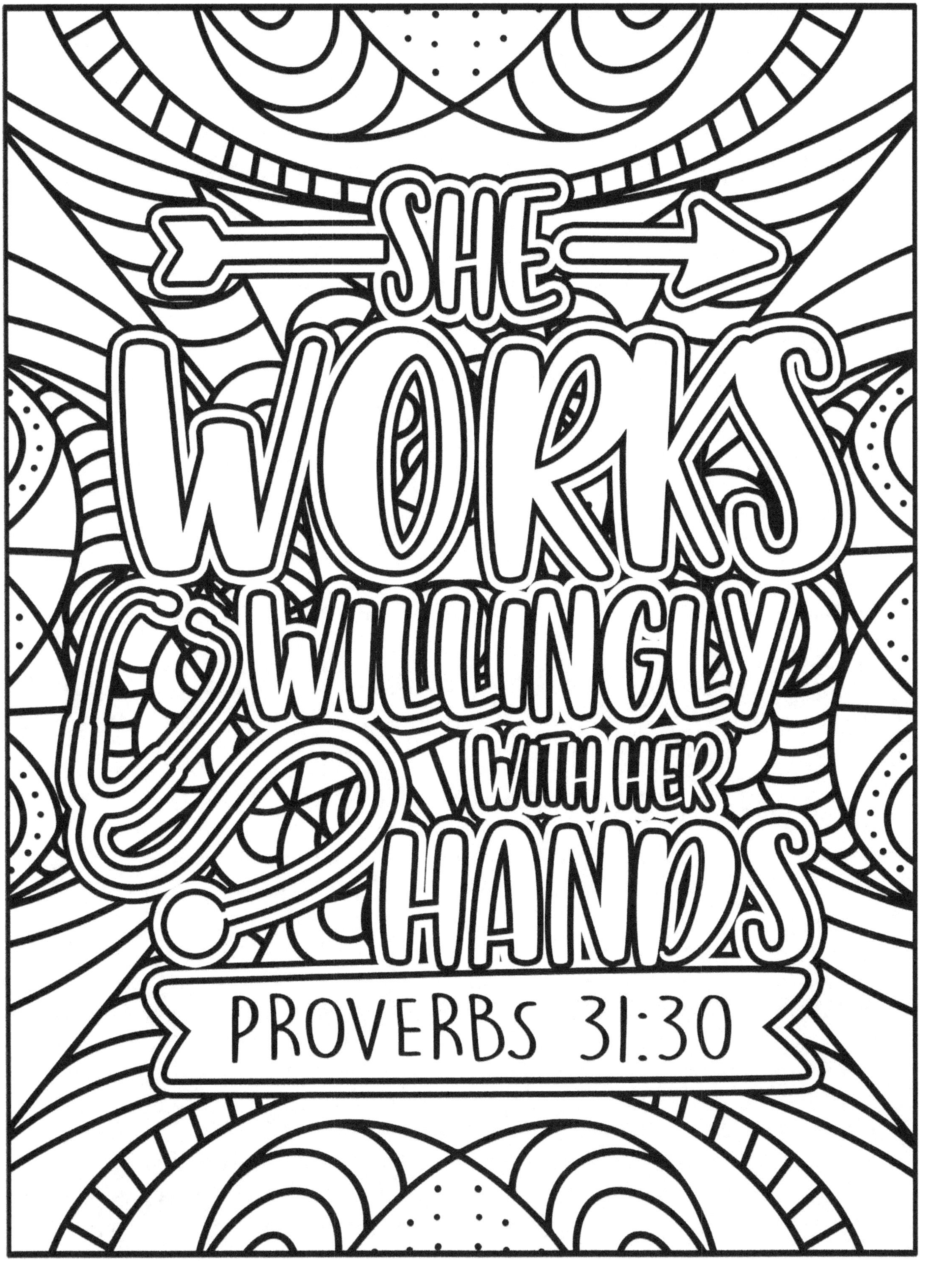
SHE
WORKS
WILLINGLY
WITH HER
HANDS
PROVERBS 31:30

JOBARTS4U

TOUGH
ENOUGH TO BE A
Nurse
CRAZY
ENOUGH TO Love IT

JOBARTS4U

ROCKIN'
the
NURSE
life

JOBARTS4U

Love
#nurselife

JOBARTS4U

Made in the USA
Las Vegas, NV
06 December 2022

60879639R00037